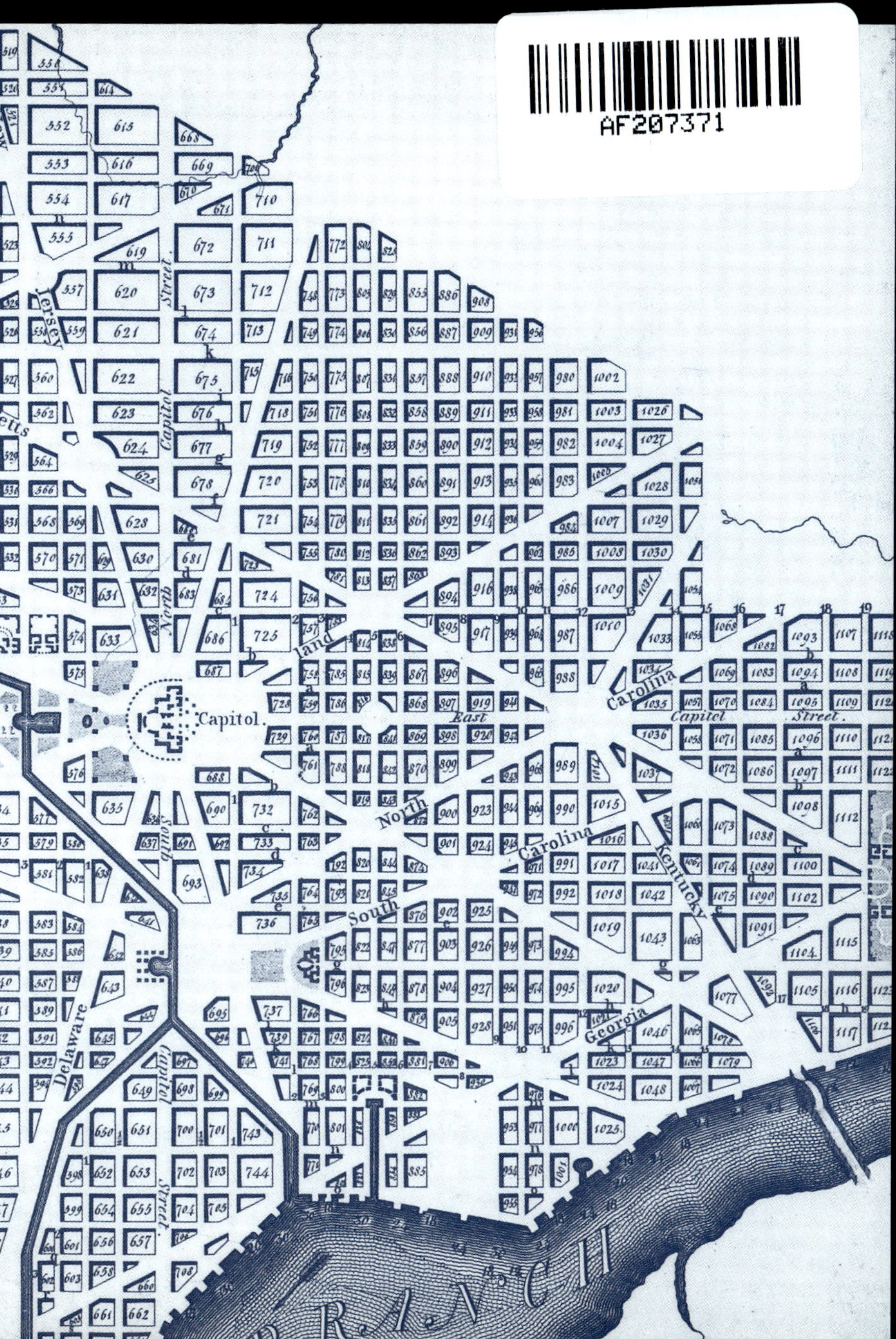

New Jersey
Massachusetts
Capitol Street
North
Capitol
Maryland
Delaware
South
Capitol Street
North Carolina
South Carolina
East Capitol Street
Carolina
Kentucky
Georgia
BRANCH

WASHINGTON LANDMARKS

A Collection of Architecture and Historical Details

Charles J. Ziga
Annie Lise Roberts

Photography by
Charles J. Ziga

DOVETAIL
BOOKS

For our parents

WASHINGTON LANDMARKS

Contents

"I see the capital city as something…more than a place to live and work….
I see it as a symbol….I think we should plan now with the realization
that a great nation is going to rise on this continent….
Right now, we have a chance which no nation has ever given itself….
How can America plan for less than greatness?"

PIERRE CHARLES L'ENFANT

L'Enfant's Federal City
A City of Magnificent Distances

Choosing a site for the capital of the newly independent nation was a political challenge. The Continental Congress meet in various cities before a permanent location in the south was negotiated. President Washington selected the rural area along the Potomac River and appointed **Pierre Charles L'Enfant** as *City Planner* and *Architect* of public buildings. The French emigré had fought under Washington and subsequently worked in New York City, establishing himself as an architect. Pierre Charles L'Enfant, George Washington, and Thomas Jefferson shared a vision for a great capital rising along the Potomac River, unprecedented in scale and grandeur —a city of magnificent distances.

L'Enfant selected Jenkins Hill, the area's highest plateau, the the Capitol. What better monument for the new republic than the building deemed by Thomas Jefferson "the first temple dedicated to the sovereignty of the people." L'Enfant's city plan linked the Capitol (then called Congress House) to the President's House via a grand avenue (Pennsylvania Avenue), the first of a diagonal grid of avenues superimposed over a rectilinear grid of streets. The avenues linked key government buildings and the intersections created neighborhood parks for statues and monuments. L'Enfant's idea for a city with great vistas and monumental buildings was inspired by *Baroque* city planning popular in Europe at the time.

Because the Federal City was designed to be a showcase for democracy, the architecture of ancient Greece was adopted. *Classical* architecture, in its many variations, still dominates the city. Despite a shared vision, L'Enfant proved too difficult to work with and was dismissed. Although he worked on the project for only one year, it is L'Enfant's plan that has shaped and guided the city's development. **Andrew Ellicott,** *Surveyor,* drew the plan based on L'Enfant's sketches and notes.

The task of building the capital was formidable; funds and materials were scarce and skilled workers were unwilling to move into the undeveloped area. There were many setbacks, including the burning of the Capitol and the President's House in 1814 by the British. By the 1870s, the city finally emerged as a nation's capital when **Alexander Shepherd,** *Vice President of Public Works,* paved over 180 miles of streets, planted 6,000 trees, and constructed sidewalks. But the ongoing discussion of relocating the Federal City did not cease until the State, War, and Navy Building (Old Executive Office Building) was completed in 1888.

At the turn of the century, the Commission of Fine Arts and the McMillian Commission, headed by **Daniel Burnham,** *Architect,* were established to plan the Mall and guide future planning of the capital. The commissions revived L'Enfant's city plan and encouraged the return to *Classical* architecture popularized by the Chicago Columbia Exposition of 1893. Due largely to their efforts, the capital today looks much as was envisioned by the original city planners more than 200 years ago.

White House

The President's House
1600 PENNSYLVANIA AVENUE, N.W.

The architecture of the White House embraced the new spirit and classicism of a national architecture promoted by Washington and Jefferson. By using cut stone, rather than brick, a precedent was established for a scale and formality appropriate for public buildings. The use of stone also signified a break from the brick-style *Georgian* architecture associated with King George of England.

James Hoban, *Architect,* Irish American, self-taught master builder. He won the commission, $500, and a city lot. Hoban's design recalls a graceful manor house featuring a central Ionic portico and hipped roof surmounted by a balustrade.

The cornerstone was laid in 1792 and work proceeded slowly due to lack of funds and a shortage of skilled craftsmen willing to move to the undeveloped capital. When President John Adams and First Lady Abigail occupied the residence in 1800, the interior was far from complete, much less furnished. A shanty town of laborers' shacks and dirt roads surrounded the incomplete presidential residence.

The most famous residence in the United States is over 200 years old and has undergone numerous renovations, additions, and modernization. It was not uncommon for a president to auction all the furnishings from previous presidencies in order to raise funds for redecorating or building. Thomas Jefferson, whose competition submission for the White House in 1791 had been rejected, was able to incorporate some of his architectural ideas during his presidency. Jefferson hired **Benjamin Latrobe,** *British Architect and Engineer,* to design the low colonnaded east and west wings. After the British burned the building in 1814, Latrobe rebuilt the damaged residence and later designed the north porte cochere and the semicircular south portico. As the sandstone became discolored by the fire, the White House was painted white, thus earning its name. During President Truman's administration, it was structurally necessary to completely rebuild the interior with a new foundation and steel framework at a cost of over $5,000,000. In the 1960s, First Lady Jacqueline Kennedy recovered many of the original furnishings and artifacts from previous administrations and renovated the interior to a glory befitting the president's house.

"I pray Heaven to bestow the best of blessings
on this house and on all that shall hereafter
.inhabit it. May none but honest and wise men
ever rule under this roof."

JOHN ADAMS
1800

"The Capitol is the first temple dedicated
to the sovereignty of the people, embellishing with
Athenian taste the course of a nation looking far
beyond the range of Athenian destinies."

THOMAS JEFFERSON
1812

UNITED STATES CAPITOL
Congress House
CAPITOL HILL, BETWEEN CONSTITUTION AVENUE AND INDEPENDENCE AVENUE

Pierre Charles L'Enfant chose Jenkins Hill as the site for the Capitol because it was "a pedestal waiting for a monument." The United States Capitol symbolizes the spirit and essence of the nation's democracy. Members of Congress, elected by the people, meet in the Senate and House of Representatives to write laws governing the country. The building of the Capitol required seventy years and numerous building phases from the time President Washington laid the cornerstone in 1793. In fact, the building of the Capitol parallels the turbulent history of the young democracy; construction was frequently interrupted by wars, lack of monies and the time-consuming democratic process.

Dr. William Thornton, *amateur Architect,* won the competition and a $500 award. Thornton oversaw construction until 1803.

Benjamin H. Latrobe, *British Architect and Engineer,* was appointed to complete the Capitol expeditiously. Latrobe modified Thornton's design after the British set fire to the Capitol in 1814. The columns, with their uniquely American motifs of tobacco leaf and corn stalk capitals, are attributed to Latrobe.

Charles Bulfinch, *Architect,* was appointed in 1817. He built a modified version of Thornton's design for the central pavilion linking the House and Senate wings, which had stood as separate buildings for years. With its Corinthian columns, simple pediment and low dome, the pavilion was reminiscent of the Pantheon in Rome.

Thomas U. Walter, *Architect,* designed and built the House and Senate extensions and the existing 180-foot-tall dome. Walter's dome, a double shell made of cast-iron and weighing more than nine million pounds, was an engineering feat of the 1850s.

Freedom, the bronze female statue that crowns the dome is 19½ feet tall and was designed by **Thomas Crawford.** At the statue's base are inscribed the Latin words *E Pluribus Unum* (from many, one).

The Octagon

OCTAGON HOUSE
American Institute of Architects Headquarters
1799 NEW YORK AVENUE, N.W.

Wanting to encourage development in the young capital, George Washington persuaded his friend Colonel John Tayloe III to build a winter residence in the young city. At the time, the Federal "city" was still a rural village with muddy streets. The Octagon, when completed in 1801, was one of the first brick residences built in the city. It was the center of society life and many of the capital's most influential people were entertained there.

The street pattern, although undeveloped, was established by L'Enfant's plan when Tayloe bought the triangular-shaped lot for $1,000. Tayloe commissioned **Dr. William Thornton,** *the first Architect of the Capitol,* to design the house. Thornton's design is remarkable for the plan, and the resulting volume that reflects the 70-degree triangular-shaped site created by New York Avenue and 18th Street. The Octagon is really a hexagon with a rounded entry pavilion. Despite the unusual lot shape, the residence adheres to the simplicity and elegance of *Federal* architecture. The brick house has three stories of different heights; the overall building height was limited to what the fire equipment could reach at the time. The second story has a stone course and between the second- and third-floor windows are stone inset panels. In the rounded pavilion, at the streets' intersection, the front door is crowned with an elliptical glass fanlight.

When the British burned the White House and Capitol in 1814, the Octagon House was spared because it was occupied by the French Ambassador. While the White House was being rebuilt, President James Madison and First Lady Dolley lived at the house for six months. During their stay, the *Treaty of Ghent* was signed, ending the War of 1812 with the British.

The American Institute of Architects purchased the building for use as its headquarters in 1902 at a cost of $30,000. The house has been painstakingly restored using traditional techniques of the original period. Furnished and decorated in the original manor style, the building is open to the public as a museum. It is said that the ghost of Colonel Tayloe's daughter (who killed herself at the residence) roams throughout the house and grounds.

Department of the Treasury
In God We Trust

Established in 1789 as a department of the executive branch, the Treasury holds and distributes the nation's funds. The Secretary of the Treasury is the second-highest-ranking executive cabinet member after the Secretary of State. Once the executive branch determines the government's yearly budget, Congress approves the budget and directs the Treasury on allocating the nation's funds. Departments of the Treasury include Bureau of Customs, U.S. Secret Service, Bureau of Engraving and Printing, Internal Revenue Service, and Bureau of Mint.

Located to the east of the White House, the present Treasury is the third to occupy the site; both former Treasury buildings were lost to fire. President Andrew Jackson selected the site and in 1836 construction began on the east wing.

During the 33 years of construction, four of Washington's most prominent architects worked on the building. **Robert B. Mills** designed the original E-shaped building but was dismissed after finishing only the east wing. Mills also designed the Washington Monument and the Old Patent Office Building. When the south wing (shown) was built, designed by **Ammi B. Young,** it interrupted the prominent Pennsylvania Avenue axis linking the White House and the Capitol. This was the first major divergence from L'Enfant's city plan. The west wing was completed in 1864 by **Isaiah Rogers**. The architect of the Old Executive Office Building, **Alfred B. Mullet,** completed the north wing in 1869.

Occupying two city blocks, the building is considered one of the finest examples of *Greek Revival* architecture in the country. The fireproof structure is the third-oldest governmental building after the White House and the Capitol. Currently, the building houses the administration offices of the Treasury Department.

The statues of Alexander Hamilton, *first Secretary of the Treasury (1789–95),* on the south plaza and Albert Gallatin, *fourth Secretary of the Treasury (1801–14),* on the north plaza are by **James E. Fraser,** *Sculptor* (also designer of the old Buffalo nickel). The Treasury Building is pictured on the back of $10 bills.

"A national debt, if it is not excessive,
will be to us a national blessing."

ALEXANDER HAMILTON
1781

"Every man is a valuable member of society who by
his observations, researches, and experiments,
procures knowledge for men.... It is in his knowledge
that man has found his greatness and his happiness."

JAMES SMITHSON

SMITHSONIAN INSTITUTION
The Castle
1000 JEFFERSON DRIVE, S.W.

James **Smithson,** *English Scientist and Benefactor,* who had never seen America, bequeathed his fortune "To found at Washington, under the name of the Smithsonian Institution, an establishment for the increase and diffusion of knowledge among men." His gift of gold sovereigns worth more than $500,000 was received in 1835 after his only living heir died.

First chartered in 1846 by Congress, the Smithsonian Institution has expanded to become the largest and most diversified museum complex in the world with collections of artifacts and specimens numbering over 100 million. Its annual budget for the acquisition and propagation of historical, cultural, and scientific knowledge is approximately $320 million. The complex of museums attracts more visitors than any tourist center in the nation.

Joseph Henry, *the Smithsonian's first secretary,* was one of the most distinguished scientists in the mid-1800s.

James Renwick, Jr., *Architect,* also designed the Renwick Gallery, the Oak Hill Cemetery chapel, and Saint Patrick's Cathedral in New York.

Begun in 1847 and completed eight years later, the *Romanesque* castle marked the beginning of a 50-year departure from the formality of *Classical* architecture toward the romanticism of *Gothic* and *Romanesque.* The Smithsonian's first director, Joseph Henry, established the architectural design criteria as functionality, flexibility, and cost effectiveness. The resulting building is asymmetrical and articulated; the lack of sculptural and decorative details is compensated by its towers, belfries, turrets, pinnacles, arched windows, and battlemented cornice. The red sandstone castle is the only building interrupting the rectangular shape of the Mall.

"The Castle" has come to symbolize the Smithsonian Institution. The 90-room building houses the Smithsonian Information Center, the Smithsonian's administrative offices, and the Woodrow Wilson International Center for Scholars. James Smithson's tomb is located adjacent to the north entrance vestibule.

WASHINGTON MONUMENT
The Father of Our Country
15TH STREET AND CONSTITUTION AVENUE, N.W.

The 555-foot-high white marble obelisk is the city's most prominent landmark. Rising from a grassy knoll on the Mall, it is the only vertical element in a horizontal city and is visible for miles. Honoring the first President of the United States, the Monument is encircled by 50 American flags and is one of the tallest masonry structures in the world.

The initial idea for a monument to George Washington dates back to the Continental Congress of 1783. Although discussed numerous times throughout the years, land for the Monument was not authorized by Congress until 1848. The original site proposed in L'Enfant's plan was the intersection of the primary axis of the White House and the Capitol. The land, however, proved too marshy and the Monument was shifted southeast to higher ground. Congress was unable to appropriate funds for the Monument so the Washington National Monument Society was founded in 1833 to raise money. Funds were donated by citizens, organizations, states, foreign countries, and the federal government.

Robert B. Mills, *Architect.* His competition-winning design called for a circular *Greco-Roman* temple with a 700-foot-high shaft. It was later altered by others due to insufficient funds. He also designed the east wing of the Treasury Building.

During the Civil War, construction was interrupted and the truncated 150-foot-high monument stood unfinished for years, reflecting the nation's fragmentation. The slight change in marble coloration shows where construction was resumed. Adjustments were also made to the proportions of the obelisk to match those of ancient Egyptian obelisks (ten times higher than wide). The monument was finally dedicated in 1885 and opened to the public three years later.

The hollow obelisk tapers as it rises, ending in an aluminum capstone. The walls are 15 feet thick at the base and 10 inches thick at the top. Lining the walls of the stairway are 190 carved memorial stones (inset) donated by states, foreign nations, organizations, and people in lieu of money. The monument was completed at a cost of $1,500,000. Its approximate weight is 90,000 tons.

"The preservation of the sacred fire of liberty, and the
destiny of the republican model of government, are justly
considered as deeply, perhaps as finally staked, on the
experiment entrusted to the hands of the American people."

GEORGE WASHINGTON
First Inaugural Address, 1789

DEDICATED TO ART.
THE RENWICK GALLERY
Dedicated to American Art
QUILTS
QUILTS

RENWICK GALLERY
Dedicated to Art
PENNSYLVANIA AVENUE AND SEVENTEENTH STREET, N.W.

The Renwick Gallery was the original home of the Corcoran collection. It was the first building in Washington designed specifically to be a museum and was the first major example of *French Second Empire* architecture in the United States. Today, the museum is part of the Smithsonian Institution and features American crafts of the 20th century.

William Wilson Corcoran, *Financier, Philanthropist,* commissioned Renwick to design the gallery in 1858. He was the first art collector to bequeath a private art collection for use in a public museum.

James Renwick, Jr., *Architect,* was considered one of the leading architects of the 19th century. The *French Second Empire* style, exemplified by the Louvre in Paris, greatly influenced Washington's architecture; it spearheaded a brief departure from the dominant *Classical* architecture constructed of stone.

During the Civil War, before construction was completed, the building was seized and occupied by the Union Army. After the war, when returned to Corcoran, a southern sympathizer, the museum's trustees successfully sued the government for back rent. The museum finally opened in 1871 with a gala ball to benefit the Washington Monument's building fund. After only 26 years, the collection outgrew the gallery. Corcoran built his second gallery of art and sold the original building for $300,000 to the U.S. Claims Court. In the 1960s the Kennedy administration campaigned to save the building from demolition. It was renovated, renamed the Renwick Gallery after its architect, and reopened in 1972.

The two-story brick building is rectangular with slightly articulated corner pavilions and a curved mansard roof with filigreed ironwork. To either side of the entrance are sculpted wreaths containing artist's brushes and sculptor's tools. In the central pediment, above the inscription *Dedicated to Art,* is a bronze relief portrait of Corcoran. Originally, the second story had niches with statues of noted artists, sculptors, and architects. Only two of the niches remain today, with statues of Nurillo and Rubens (inset). The others were replaced with windows.

CORCORAN GALLERY OF ART

For the Encouragement of American Genius

17TH STREET AND NEW YORK AVENUE, N.W.

The Corcoran Gallery of Art was founded in 1859 by William Wilson Corcoran "for the encouragement of American genius." The privately endowed gallery was the capital's first, and for many years, largest art museum. Dedicated to the development and display of American artists, the museum's American art collection is one of the world's finest. Housed for 26 years at what is now called the Renwick Gallery, the collection and school moved to the new Corcoran Gallery of Art in 1879.

Ernest Flagg, *Architect,* a recent graduate of the Ecole des Beaux-Arts in Paris, was commissioned to design the new museum, which was completed nine years after Corcoran's death.

Above the rusticated first floor is a great expanse of Georgian marble interrupted only by the entry pediment. Over the front door is inscribed the Corcoran motto, *Dedicated to Art.* The semicircular wing of the *Beaux-Arts* building is an amphitheater that gracefully accommodates the difficult trapezoidal site created by the intersections of 17th Street and New York Avenue. To each side of the stair are bronze lions—replicas of those at Saint Peter's in Rome. Other details include ornamental grillwork and an inscribed frieze below an elaborate copper roof. The names on the frieze are of world-renowned artists.

The first floor is dominated by a pair of two-story atriums skylit from above. On either side of the grand marble staircase, leading to the second-floor galleries, are platforms originally designed for displaying casts of classical sculpture. The collection includes works from every major period of American art as well as an impressive collection of the European masters. The gallery's permanent collection has more than 11,000 objects.

"The best building designed in Washington."

FRANK LLOYD WRIGHT

*"Science is the pursuit above all which impresses us
with the capacity of man for intellectual and
moral progress and awakens the human intellect to
aspiration for a higher condition of humanity."*

JOSEPH HENRY,
Smithsonian Institution's First Secretary, 1846–78

ARTS AND INDUSTRIES BUILDING
The Nation's Attic
900 JEFFERSON DRIVE, S.W.

The Arts and Industries Building was the country's first National Museum. It was built to house exhibits from the Philadelphia Centennial of 1876, the first World's Fair held in the United States. Foreign governments and state agencies eliminated the costly expense of return shipping by donating the exhibits to the U.S. government. Congress appropriated $250,000 to build the National Museum. Its opening was celebrated in conjunction with President Garfield's inaugural ball in March, 1881.

The architecture of the building, as well as the exhibits it contains, celebrate the Industrial Revolution of the Victorian era. Over 60 freight cars of exhibits containing items such as horse-drawn carriages, pocket watches, chamber-room furniture, and a wood-burning locomotive were donated to the Smithsonian. The eclectic collection expanded the Smithsonian Institute's areas of study to include historical and technological fields as well as natural history. The exhibits increased the Smithsonian's holdings fourfold and established the institution as the nation's depository of cultural artifacts, thereby earning its nickname *The Nation's Attic.*

Aldoph Cluss and **Paul Schulze,** *Architects.*

The polychrome brick building is square and symmetrical in plan with a central skylit rotunda and radiating turreted wings. A pair of towers frame the main entrance and to either side are wings with continuous arches terminated by corner pavilions. The spacious interior is flooded by natural light. Iron stairways and balconies lead to mezzanines within the 56-foot-high space. The building's structural trusses and mechanical systems are exposed to view, complimenting this eclectic collection from the era of the Industrial Revolution.

The sculpture above the building's main entry is *Columbia Protecting Science and Industry* by **Casper Buberl,** *Sculptor.*

The sandstone-and-brick building was restored in celebration of the Philadelphia Bicentennial in 1974–76 by **Hugh Newell Jacobsen,** *Architect.*

"*I don't want it torn down.
I think it's the greatest monstrosity in America.*"

HARRY S. TRUMAN
1958

OLD EXECUTIVE OFFICE BUILDING

Former State, War and Navy Building

PENNSYLVANIA AVENUE AND 17TH STREET, N.W.

The Old Executive Office Building (OEOB) was built for the State, War, and Navy Departments. Construction began under the Grant Administration reflecting the optimistic and opulent building period in Washington following the Civil War. Its enormous size and cost of $10 million ($9.5 million over budget) settled the ongoing discussion of relocating the nation's capital to a different city. Even before completion, the building's architectural style was scorned by many as un-American and not in the spirit of the nation's capital. Today it is considered one of the finest examples of *French Second Empire* architecture in the country.

Alfred B. Mullet, *Architect.* Also designed the north wing of the Treasury Building as well as many post offices and custom houses in the U.S.
Richard von Ezdorf, *Architect.* Responsible for many resplendent interior details.

The enormous mass is articulated by porches, porticos, and 900 Tuscan columns. Five stories of columns are crowned by a mansard roof with dormers. Its wings, constructed in stages, were occupied by the military departments as they were being finished, finally resulting in a rectangle shaped building with two inner courtyards. When completed after 17 years of construction in 1888, it was Washington's largest office building with over 500 rooms, ten acres of floor space, and two miles of marble hallways. Designed to be fireproof, the structure was built with granite, marble, cast iron, and plaster. The exterior granite walls are four-and-a-half feet thick.

The most notable and elegant rooms are the four-story White House Library and Research Center with white cast iron balconies and a Minton tile floor; the Indian Treaty Room (site of over 900 treaty signings) with marble wall panels and sculptural bronze lamps; and the White House Law Library, designed in an eclectic mix of *Moorish, Baroque,* and *Gothic* architectural styles.

The building was spared several attempts at demolition and renovations throughout the years (as recently as 1957) primarily due to lack of funds. Demolition alone would cost more than constructing a new building. A complete restoration began under the Kennedy administration. The executive branch took occupancy in 1949 and the building was renamed the Executive Office Building.

NATIONAL BUILDING MUSEUM

Old Pension Building

FIFTH AND F STREETS, N.W.

Completed in 1887, the building housed the Pension Bureau, a federal agency which distributed pensions for disabled war veterans and their dependents. Its architecture was criticized as typical Victorian excessiveness and it was threatened with demolition in the 1950s. Today, the eclectic structure is finally appreciated; the building houses the National Building Museum celebrating America's building arts, traditions, and achievements.

Montgomery C. Meigs, *Quartermaster-General of the Union Army and Civil Engineer.* The West Point graduate also supervised the construction of the Arts and Industries Building and the mid-19th-century addition to the Capitol.

Constructed of more than 15 million bricks, the massive three-story building occupies an entire city block, earning its nickname "Meigs's old red barn." The facade of repetitive, pedimented windows is a copy of the 16th-century Palazzo Farnese in Rome, by Michelangelo. Soaring an additional three stories, the gabled clerestory provides light and air to the interior. Above the first-floor windows and extending around the building's 1,200-foot circumference is a three-foot-high terra-cotta frieze, designed by **Casper Buberl.** It depicts action scenes from the Civil War, including generals on horses, marching infantry and wagon trains.

Meigs's design was innovative in providing a healthy climate for office workers; the open, arcaded galleries surrounding the courtyard eliminated dark interior corridors and provided natural light and cross ventilation for open work areas and offices. Dominating the interior is a spacious courtyard with eight 75-foot-high Corinthian columns. The massive columns are eight feet in diameter and are each constructed of 85,000 bricks, plastered and painted to look like marble. Historical state and war documents, maps, and a facsimile of the *Declaration of Independence* are said to have been inserted into the columns during construction. The Great Hall has been the site of many presidential inaugural balls.

"The Pension building endures, not just as an architectural and engineering landmark, but as an embodiment of American craftsmanship and a constant reminder that we must all be ever vigilant to defend and promote the quality of our built environment."

ROBERT W. DUEMLING,
President and Director of the National Building Museum, 1989

OLD POST OFFICE
Old Tooth

The *Romanesque* building was a prestigious symbol for the United States Postal Service when completed in 1899. It was the city's first steel-frame building, fireproofed by a skin of granite stone. Mail sorting was done under the central skylit court, which measures 99 feet by 184 feet. Today, "The Pavilion," an open courtyard with shops and restaurants, is one of the largest open public spaces in the city. The 315-foot clock tower, displaying the city's most elevated clock, is Washington's third-tallest building. Open to the public, the views provide a wonderful perspective of the capital city.

W. J. Edbrooke, *Architect.* His design for the Post Office was inspired by H. H. Richardson's Allegheny Court House in Pittsburgh, Pennsylvania. The medieval-style structure, nicknamed the "Old Tooth" because of its rough-faced exterior and clock tower, was built at a cost of $2,585,000.

The building fell out of popularity shortly after its completion because its architectural style conflicted with the prevailing *Neoclassical* architecture of the Federal Triangle (area of Constitution Ave., Pennsylvania Ave., and 15th Street). In 1934, the Post Office General moved to new headquarters across the street and the building was occupied by other governmental agencies for the next 44 years. Falling into disrepair, the building was threatened with demolition in 1971. The building was saved, however, largely by the efforts of the preservationist group "Don't tear it down" and **Nancy Hawks,** *President of the National Endowment for the Arts.* Under a federal restoration project costing $30 million (less than what demolition and a new building would cost), the Old Post Office was renovated into a multi-use complex with seven floors of federal office space and three floors of commercial and public space. Re-dedicated in 1983, the project acted as a catalyst for the rehabilitation of the Pennsylvania Avenue area.

The Congress Bells, housed in the tower, were a gift from Great Britain celebrating America's bicentennial. They are rung on holidays and special occasions.

LIBRARY OF CONGRESS
Thomas Jefferson Building
10 FIRST STREET, S.E.

The library was created in 1800 to serve as a reference facility for Congress. It later opened to other members of government, and eventually to the public, becoming the largest public library in the world. Seven thousand new items are acquired every day. The library's holdings of over 90 million items are held in three principle buildings, the Thomas Jefferson Building (1897), the John Adams Building (1939), and the James Madison Memorial Building (1980).

When the British burned the capital in 1814, the original 3,000-volume library was lost; Thomas Jefferson sold his personal book collection of 6,500 volumes to Congress to reestablish the library. Today its extensive collection is the result of an 1870 amendment to the copyright law requiring two copies of every item published in the U.S. to be deposited at the library. Two thirds of the collection is in a language other than English. And a few of the more priceless items include the *Giant Bible of Mainz,* the *Gutenberg Bible,* Jefferson's first draft of the *Declaration of Independence,* President Lincoln's handwritten drafts of the *Gettysburg Address* and the *Emancipation Proclamation,* original priceless musical manuscripts, and a collection of Stradivarius stringed instruments.

John Smithmeyer and **Paul Pelz,** *Architects* of the Thomas Jefferson Building. **Thomas L. Casey,** *General of the U.S. Army Corp. of Engineers,* oversaw construction and was mainly responsible for the building's exquisite interior.

Built in 1897, the Thomas Jefferson Building was the first structure created to house the library and has come to symbolize the Library of Congress. The three-story *Italian Renaissance* building is highly articulated and adorned with paired columns, broken pediments, rustication, and garlands. On top of the low copper dome is a lantern and finial torch symbolizing the flame of knowledge. Inside, the octagonal main reading room, dominated by the 125-foot-high stained glass skylit rotunda, is one of the most opulent rooms in the city. The interior is richly decorated with sculpture, mosaics, murals, plaques, and panels, with few surfaces left unadorned. At the west front of the building is a 50-foot semicircular pool containing the *Neptune Fountain* (inset), by **Roland Hinton Perry,** *Sculptor.*

"Learned institutions ought to be favorite objects
with every free people. They throw that light over the
public mind which is the best security against crafty
and dangerous encroachments on the public liberty."

JAMES MADISON
1822

*"Remember that all of us, you and I especially,
  are descended from immigrants and revolutionists."*

FRANKLIN D. ROOSEVELT
1938

DAUGHTERS OF THE AMERICAN REVOLUTION
National Society Headquarters
1776 D STREET, N.W.

In 1890, after the Sons of the American Revolution voted to exclude women from their membership, **Mary S. Lockwood** founded the Daughters of the American Revolution (DAR) with the patronage of First Lady Caroline Harrison. DAR quickly surpassed the Sons of the American Revolution in influence and membership. Today the society has over 200,000 members, with chapters in every state as well as around the world. Potential members must establish descent from a Revolutionary War veteran who was loyal to the cause of American Independence. The society has an outstanding genealogical library and assists people in tracing their lineage.

The complex of buildings that serves as National Society Headquarters is the largest owned exclusively by women. This complex was also the site of the First Armament Limitation talks in 1921.

Edward Pearce Casey, *Architect,* designed the principal building in the complex, Memorial Continental Hall. It was built in 1910 at a cost of $500,000. At the time the site was chosen, the area was surrounded by a cow pasture and was without a streetcar stop nearby. Facing onto the President's Park Ellipse, the *Beaux-Arts* building is built of white marble and features an extended porte cochere supported by Ionic columns. To the south is a semicircular portico with 13 columns representing the original 13 states. The Hall houses 33 period rooms maintained by state chapters and are furnished and decorated in the style typical of each state's early American homes.

The museum has a renowned collection of decorative arts including china, silver, textiles, and other artifacts documenting American domestic history. Pieces of the collection include one of the only two surviving tea chests from the Boston Tea Party in 1773; a painting of the Battle of Bennington by Grandma Moses (a member of DAR); and White House china designed by First Lady Caroline Harrison.

WILLARD HOTEL

Hotel of Presidents

1401 PENNSYLVANIA AVENUE, N.W.

There has been a hotel at 1401 Pennsylvania Avenue since 1816, the present one being the sixth. The Willard Hotel has always been one of Washington's premiere social and political meeting places. After World War II, however, the Willard Hotel fell into disrepair along with the city's downtown business area. In 1968, the hotel was closed and its furnishings auctioned off; it was left vacant for over a decade. Today, restored to its original glory and protected as a National Historic Landmark, it stands as a symbol to the revitalization of Pennsylvania Avenue and Washington's downtown area.

Henry J. Hardenburgh, *Architect.* Also designed the Plaza Hotel and the Dakota apartments in New York City.

Henry Willard, *Hotelier.* He opened the old Willard Hotel in 1850 and built the present building in 1901. The Willard family controlled the hotel until 1946.

With a history of serving heads of state, dignitaries, and society's elite, the impressive list of guests included the Prince of Wales (Edward VIII), Charles Dickens, Julia Ward Howe (author of the *Battle Hymn of the Republic*), Buffalo Bill, Albert Einstein, John Philip Sousa, and Mark Twain. Ten president-elects, including Lincoln, Harding, and Pierce, stayed at the hotel prior to taking occupancy at the White House. President Ulysses Grant, while taking a rest from the presidency in the hotel's lobby, was confronted by people requesting political favors. He is credited with coining the term "lobbyist."

Built in the *Beaux-Arts* style and one of the city's first steel structures, the twelve-story building looks out upon Pershing Park. Its first three floors are of Indiana limestone and the nine remaining are constructed of pale-colored brick laid to look like rusticated masonry. The building's mansard roof has chateau-like turrets and elaborate chimney pots. On Pennsylvania Avenue, a three-story-high portico with four Doric columns marks the entrance. On the lobby's ceiling are seals of the first 48 states (inset). Alaska and Hawaii were added later to the main hallway.

"He that would bring home the wealth of the Indies
must carry the wealth of the Indies with him.
So it is in traveling. A man must carry knowledge
with him if he would bring home knowledge."

Inscription on Union Station's
Frieze to the left of the main entrance

UNION STATION
Gateway to the Nation's Capital
40 MASSACHUSETTS AVENUE, N.W.

When completed in 1907, Union Station was the largest train station in the world. It was the first building designed in accordance with the McMillian Commission's report. The report revived L'Enfant's original city plan and promoted a return to *Classical* architecture popularized after the Columbian Exposition of 1893 in Chicago. The building offers the traveler an immediate and powerful view of the Capitol from its arches.

Daniel H. Burnham, *Architect,* was instrumental in both the Columbian Exposition in Chicago and the McMillian Commission, which terminated the city's brief flirtation with Victorian architecture. He also designed the Monadnock building in Chicago and the Flatiron building in New York City.

Built between the world wars, Union Station was the city's main transportation hub for over 50 years. At its peak, over 42,000 daily travelers used the station, as well as its bowling alley, mortuary, turkish baths, and hotel. Serving as the gateway to the nation's capital, dignitaries, president-elects, and celebrities arrived by train with great celebration.

In the 1960s, air travel overtook train travel and Union Station began to fall into disrepair. The building was rescued by a $160-million renovation project and reopened in 1988. Restored to its former beauty, Union Station serves the city as a multi-use complex, with train transportation, shops, restaurants, and movie theaters.

Built of Vermont marble, the *Beaux-Arts*-style building has a central pavilion with three great arches forming the entry loggia, clearly inspired by the Arch of Constantine in Rome. Six allegorical statues, by **Louis Saint-Gaudens,** *Sculptor,* stand atop the Ionic columns that frame the arches. Flanking the central pavilion are low arcaded wings serving the trains. The interior is reminiscent of Roman baths and has a 96-foot-high barrel-vaulted ceiling with gilded octagonal coffers. From the second-floor balcony, 36 statues of Roman legionnaires (inset) watch over the flow of pedestrians.

REPUBLIC OF INDONESIA EMBASSY

Walsh-McLean House

2020 MASSACHUSETTS AVENUE, N.W.

The turn-of-the-century *Beaux-Arts* mansion was originally built as a private residence for Thomas F. Walsh. It is one of this area's many grand residences built during a time of great affluence, prior to the Great Depression. Known today as "Embassy Row," the stretch of Massachusetts Avenue, between Scott and Observation circles, houses over 50 embassies and consulates.

Thomas F. Walsh, *Gold Magnate.* In the late 1800s, the Irish immigrant discovered and owned one of the richest gold mines in the world, Camp Bird Mine in Colorado. He built the mansion in 1902–3, at a cost of $835,000. The family hosted many lavish parties, entertaining the social and political elite of Washington including Presidents Theodore Roosevelt, Taft, Wilson, and Harding. His daughter, Evalyn Walsh-McLean, was once the owner of the Hope Diamond. She sold the house to the Republic of Indonesia in 1952 for $335,000. After years of being rented and neglected, the mansion had fallen into disrepair and the embassy spent an additional $75,000 to restore it.

Henry Andersen, *Danish-born Architect,* studied at the Royal Academy of Art in Copenhagen.

The three-and-a-half story mansion is built of pale-colored brick with limestone courses and details. A tower-like bay gracefully accommodates the corner of the odd shaped lot. The building undulates with additional swells and rounded corners. Following the curvature of the building is the red tile mansard roof with elaborate chimneys and round dormer windows. Other details include limestone brackets, sculpture, and decorative grillwork at the windows. Above the doors, at the Massachusetts Avenue entrance, is a loggia with marble columns, and the 21st Street entrance has a glass and metal vaulted carriage porch.

Each of the 50 rooms inside is richly decorated with *Rococo* gilded ceilings, crystal chandeliers, wood paneling, and gold-plated hardware. The central entry hall is three stories high, with a stained glass skylight and curved double stair with a mahogany rail and balusters.

NATIONAL MUSEUM OF NATURAL HISTORY
Formerly the National Museum of History and Technology
CONSTITUTION AVENUE AND TENTH STREET, N.W.

The Smithsonian Institution's rapidly growing collection prompted Congress to authorize the construction of the Institution's third building. When completed in 1911, the National Museum of Natural History stood alone across from the only other buildings on the Mall, the Arts and Industries building, "The Castle," and the Department of Agriculture. It was the first major structure built on the Mall after the McMillian Commission's report recommending a return to L'Enfant's city plan and *Classical* architecture.

The museum houses a large and diverse collection of over 120 million specimens, including collections of mammals, reptiles, birds, fish, and insects. Humans in various geographical and cultural settings are displayed in the Cultural Regions exhibits. The Hall of Gems features the Hope Diamond; at 45.5 carats, the blue diamond is the largest in the world. Other attractions include "Uncle Beazley"—a life-size model of a triceratops—and the 13-foot-high African bush elephant in the rotunda. The research institution, one of the finest in the country, provides laboratories for anthropologists, botanists, zoologists, geologists, and paleontologists.

Hornblower and **Marshall,** *Architects.*

To each side of the main entry stair are pedestals, one displaying petrified wood and the other iron ore. The central pavilion features a portico of six Corinthian columns supporting a broken pediment. The pediment and its arched window are repeated on the four sides surrounding the dome. The far east and west wings were added in 1963–65 and the building covers 16.5 acres with more than 300,000 square feet of exhibition space.

The interior rotunda is octagonal in shape with four prominent sides and measures 80 feet in diameter. The prominent sides feature three-and-a-half story arches with three levels of open balconies supported by marble Ionic columns and a clerestory arch. The dome springs from the smaller solid sides of the rotunda and soars 124 feet above the floor.

*"Fourscore and seven years ago our fathers
brought forth on this continent, a new nation,
conceived in Liberty, and dedicated to the
proposition that all men are created equal."*

ABRAHAM LINCOLN
1863

LINCOLN MEMORIAL
The Great Emancipator
WEST MALL AT 23RD STREET, N.W.

The Memorial to the 16th president is comprised of three distinctive components: the intricately carved statue of the man, the temple-like structure with 36 columns representing the states of the Union that Lincoln fought so hard to preserve, and inscriptions from both the *Gettysburg Address* and his second inaugural speech.

Since its dedication in 1922, when a black keynote speaker was mistakenly ushered away from the dais, the Memorial has come to symbolize the ideals of free speech and equality for all. Black opera singer Marian Anderson sang at the Memorial in 1939 when barred from DAR's Constitution Hall; Martin Luther King delivered his "I Have a Dream" speech in 1963 to over 200,000 people; and many public protests, including demonstrations against the Vietnam War, have been staged at this site.

Henry Bacon, *Architect.*
Daniel Chester French, *Sculptor.* Leading sculptor of public works of the time.
Jules Guerin, *Muralist,* painted the murals between the inscriptions.

Efforts to erect a Memorial to Abraham Lincoln began shortly after his assassination in 1867, but controversy over design and location delayed action until 1901 when the McMillian Commission choose the site, appointed the artists, and appropriated nearly $3 million. Construction finally began in 1915 and the monument was dedicated in 1922. The McMillian Commission extended the Mall to include the marshland up to the Potomac river, thus creating the most powerful axis in Washington; elevated on marble terraces, the Memorial counterbalances the Capitol on top of Jenkins Hill, with the elongated reflecting pool, the Washington Monument, and the great expanse of the Mall between the two buildings.

The Memorial is fashioned after the Parthenon in Greece, but departs from the classical temple form in two significant ways: the entrance is on the broad side and the pedimented roof is absent. Within the colonnaded temple, the statue of a pensive and somber Lincoln gazes out over the Mall. He is seated in a throne-like chair draped with an American flag. The 19-foot-high statue, carved out of 28 blocks of interlocked Georgian marble, took the marble cutters—the Piccarilli Brothers— four years to complete.

WASHINGTON NATIONAL CATHEDRAL
Cathedral Church of Saint Peter and Saint Paul
MASSACHUSETTS AND WISCONSIN AVENUES, N.W.

The idea for a National Cathedral dates back to when Pierre Charles L'Enfant and George Washington proposed "a great church for national purposes." Although administered by the Episcopal Church, it is considered the nation's cathedral for people of all religious faiths.

Reverend Dr. Yates Satterlee, *the first Bishop of the cathedral,* was instrumental in realizing the project. In 1893, Congress established the Protestant Episcopal Cathedral Foundation but did not authorize funds for construction. Under Satterlee's leadership, the foundation raised money, bought 57 acres on Mt. Saint Alban and built the cathedral. He also established the underlying philosophy of the cathedral welcoming all faiths and nationalities.

George F. Bodley and **Henry Vaughan,** *Architects,* were responsible for the overall design of the 14th-century *English Gothic* cathedral. As requested by Satterlee, only original Gothic building techniques were used, including flying buttresses, arches, and vaults without steel.

Philip F. Frohman, *Architect,* succeeded the original architects. He dedicated 50 years to overseeing construction and refining the original design.

George A. Fuller, *Builder.* His company worked on the structure for 83 years, maintaining artisans knowledgeable in 14th-century building techniques.

In 1907, the first stone was laid by President Theodore Roosevelt; in 1990, after 80 years of construction, the final building stone was laid by President Bush. Many national and world religious leaders have preached at the cathedral and more than 100 prominent Americans are buried in the crypt. The cathedral has been the site for expressing national grief; here, burial services were conducted for Presidents Wilson and Eisenhower, Generals Bradly and MacArthur, as well as United States service men killed in the Vietnam War.

The last Gothic church of this scale to be built, it is the sixth-largest cathedral in the world.

SUPREME COURT OF THE UNITED STATES

Equal Justice under Law

EAST CAPITOL AND FIRST STREETS, N.E.

The Supreme Court is the highest tribunal in the United States, establishing precedent for all lower courts by interpreting the Constitution and the nation's laws. As the third branch of government, it counterbalances the authority of the executive and legislative branches. The eight Associate Justices and one Chief Justice are appointed by the President and confirmed by the Senate. The court heard its first case in 1790; today, it hears approximately 170 cases out of the 5,000 petitioned annually.

John Marshall, *fourth Chief Justice, 1801–35,* is considered one of the great Chief Justices of the Supreme Court. Under his tenure, the Supreme Court's authority to declare an act of Congress or the executive branch unconstitutional was affirmed.

William Howard Taft, *Twenty-sixth President* and *tenth Chief Justice,* convinced Congress to build a permanent home for the Supreme Court in 1928.

Cass Gilbert, *Architect.* He also designed the U.S. Custom House and the Woolworth Building in New York City.

Completed in 1935, the Supreme Court's first permanent home is an adaptation of a Greek temple showing deference to the earlier democracy. Built of white marble, the central portico has massive Corinthian columns supporting a sculptured pediment. The capitals of the columns are of corn stalks, a uniquely American variation found throughout Washington architecture. To each side of the central temple are lower, unarticulated marble wings. Flanking the monumental marble stairway are seated statues representing *The Contemplation of Justice* and *The Authority of Law* (inset) by **James E. Fraser,** *Sculptor.*

Large bronze doors lead to a long, stately hall lined with Ionic columns and busts of previous Chief Justices. In the courtroom, four Ionic columns and red velvet curtains serve as a backdrop to the mahogany bench where the Justices hear oral arguments. The Chief Justice sits in the center with the Associate Justices seated by seniority to each side. The 30-foot-high ceiling is painted with friezes of allegorical figures.

"The people made the Constitution,
and the people can unmake it.
It is the creature of their own will,
and lives only by their will."

Chief Justice John Marshall
Cohens v. Virginia, 1821

NATIONAL ARCHIVES
National Archives and Records Administration
EIGHTH STREET AND CONSTITUTION AVENUE, N.W.

The National Archives was built to safeguard the nation's most treasured documents including the *Bill of Rights*, the *Constitution*, and the *Declaration of Independence*. Completed in 1937, the fireproof repository insured a safe haven for documents formerly kept by departments and often lost or damaged by fire or neglect. The massive limestone building evokes a sense of endurance and awe.

John Russell Pope, *Architect*, the leading proponent of *Neoclassical* architecture, also designed the Jefferson Memorial and the National Gallery of Art.

Built as part of the Federal Triangle Project, it was formerly the site of Center Market, the heart of the city's business life through the 1920s. The marshy land required 8,500 concrete piers, each 21 feet deep, to support the building. The rectangular building has large unbroken wall surfaces, including a massive two-tiered attic. Each facade features a portico with 57-foot-high Corinthian columns, and the north and south columns support sculptured pediments. Flanking the monumental stairs at Constitution Avenue are allegorical statues representing *Heritage* and *Guardianship* by **James E. Fraser,** *Sculptor.* The massive bronze doors, measuring 49 feet high and weighing ten tons apiece, are said to be the largest in the world.

The Charters of Freedom (*Declaration of Independence, Bill of Rights*, and the *Constitution*) are displayed on a marble dais within the semicircular hall. Kept in helium-filled bronze-and-glass cases, the documents are lowered at night into a 50-ton vault made of concrete and steel, 20 feet below the floor. To each side are murals painted by **Barry Faulkner** in 1930, portraying the signing of the *Declaration of Independence* and the ratification of the *Constitution*. The 75-foot-high space features a half dome with a coffered ceiling. The rose-and-gray Tennessee marble floor is inlaid with bronzed winged figures representing the four division of the archives: Legislation, History, Judiciary, and War and Defense. Today, the archives hold photographs, film and sound recordings, private letters, journals, and photo albums, as well as paper documents.

"This building holds in trust the records of
our national life and symbolizes our faith in
the permanency of our national institutions."

NATIONAL ARCHIVES
WESTERN FRIEZE

*"The giver of this building has matched the richness of
his gift with the modesty of his spirit, stipulating that the Gallery
shall be known not by his name but by the Nation's."*

Franklin D. Roosevelt,
1941

NATIONAL GALLERY OF ART
West Building
SIXTH STREET AND CONSTITUTION AVENUE, N.W.

The museum documents the development of 13th- to 20th-century Western art and features masterpieces exclusively. Designed after the 1893 Columbian Exposition in Chicago, it is regarded as the city's last great *Neoclassical* building.

Andrew Mellon, *Steel Magnate* and *Secretary of the Treasury (1921–32),* conceived and financed the museum as a gift to the American people. Mellon banned works of living artists, reserving the museum for the great masters of the past. The Pittsburgh millionaire donated the gallery's first collection of paintings and sculpture. When the museum opened in 1941, his collection occupied very little of the five-and-a-half acres of floor space; museum guards are said to have used one of the cavernous galleries as a basketball court. Mellon had the foresight to request the site east of the museum be reserved for future expansion and with subsequent gifts from private art collectors, the museum's holdings outgrew the building in only 30 years. Although administered as a national museum by the Smithsonian Institution, the building's initial cost of $15 million and all the art has been privately donated.

John Russell Pope, *Architect,* an avid proponent of *Neoclassical* architecture, designed 14 buildings in Washington, including the Thomas Jefferson Memorial. Although well liked by the public when the palatial museum opened in 1941, the architecture was criticized by artists and architects as neglecting current building technologies and modern aesthetics.

Facing onto the Mall, the symmetrical 758-foot-long building is massive. The facade is windowless and articulated only by simple pilasters and portals. One of the largest marble structures in the world, it is constructed of five shades of pink Tennessee marble. The central entry, inspired by the Pantheon in Rome, has an entry portico, a simple pediment, and a marble dome. With little ornamentation, the interior is equally austere and is impressive for its size, proportions, and choice of materials. The central rotunda measures 100 feet in diameter and the coffered dome is 100 feet high. Dark green marble columns supporting the dome surround the central court's fountain containing a bronze statue of Mercury (inset).

THOMAS JEFFERSON MEMORIAL
The Author of the Declaration of Independence
EAST BASIN DRIVE, S.W.

The pristine white marble Memorial is an adaptation of the Pantheon in Rome, reflecting the third president's love of *Classical* architecture. Situated on the south bank of the tidal basin, surrounded by flowering cherry trees, the Memorial aligns with the White House's north-south axis. Jefferson was instrumental in planning the Federal City and it is appropriate that his Memorial was designed in accordance with L'Enfant's, Washington's, and his own vision for a city of great vistas and monuments.

John Russell Pope, *Architect,* and avid proponent of *Neoclassical* architecture, modeled the building after Jefferson's own architectural designs, Monticello and the rotunda at the University of Virginia. Pope died before the Memorial was constructed and his associates **Otto Eggers** and **Daniel Higgins,** *Architects,* built the Memorial, but at half the size of the original design.

A congressional commission was established in 1934 to build the Memorial, which was dedicated on Jefferson's 200th birthday, April 13, 1943. The project was controversial from its inception; the location was contested, the architectural style was considered outdated, and funds were scarce during the dire economic times of the Depression. The land was originally a tidal marsh requiring concrete and steel piers 135 feet long to support the building.

Marble stairs from the tidal basin lead to the portico, which supports a sculptured pediment. The open-air-rotunda and the dome are supported by 54 Ionic columns. Inside, four marble wall panels are inscribed with excerpts from Jefferson's most powerful writings on human liberties, including excerpts from the *Declaration of Independence* and admonitions against slavery. Raised on a six-foot black granite pedestal is a 19-foot-high bronze statue of Jefferson addressing the Continental Congress. **Rudulph Evans,** *Sculptor,* won the commission through a competition entered by over 100 sculptors. As metals were scarce during World War II, a plaster statue was substituted until bronze was available again after the war.

"We hold these truths to be self-evident:
that all men are created equal, that they
are endowed by their Creator with certain
inalienable rights, among these are life,
liberty, and the pursuit of happiness."

DECLARATION OF INDEPENDENCE, 1776

*"The international organization of
the twenty-one American Republics."*

INSCRIPTION ON ENTRY PEDESTAL

Organization of American States
Pan-American Union
Constitution Avenue and 17th Street, N.W.

The Organization of American States (OAS) was established in 1948 to promote peace, economic development, and hemispheric solidarity among the independent nations of Latin America, the Caribbean, and North America. Originally called the International Union of American Republics and established in 1890, it is the oldest coalition of nations in the world. The United States was a charter member and today there are 33 member nations in the organization.

The site was donated and deemed international territory by the U.S. government and **Andrew Carnegie** contributed three-quarters of the $1,100,000 construction cost.

Paul Cret and **Albert Kelsey,** *Architects,* were awarded the commission for their competition-winning design. Cret also designed the Folger Shakespeare Library.

The *Beaux-Arts* building evokes a Spanish villa with a combination of North and South American details. An elevated marble patio leads to the triple-arched entry with decorative bronze gates. Flanking the arches are allegorical statues representing South America and North America (inset), sculpted by **Isidor Konti** and **Gutzon Borglum,** sculptor of Mount Rushmore. At the street is a bronze statue of Queen Isabella I of Spain, the financier of Columbus's voyage.

The interior is built of white Georgian marble and Andean granite and features a Spanish-style skylit courtyard filled with tropical trees and plants. The central pink marble fountain is decorated with Aztec designs. Next to the fountain is the Peace Tree, a rubber tree and fig tree grafted together, representing the America's peaceful unification. It was planted by President Taft in 1910 to commemorate the building's competition.

The Hall of Americas on the second floor has a two-story barrel-vaulted ceiling with Tiffany chandeliers and stained glass arched windows that look out upon a garden and the Museum of Modern Art of Latin America.

John F. Kennedy Center

For the Performing Arts

New Hampshire Avenue and Rock Creek Parkway

Although the idea for a national cultural center dates back to President George Washington, it was not until 1958 that Congress appropriated land and established a commission, but no funding, for the project. In 1964, when the cultural center was designated as a memorial to the slain President John F. Kennedy, donations for construction were plentiful, including gifts of art and furnishings from foreign governments.

Construction began in 1964 and the Center for the Performing Arts opened in 1971, filling the void for a much-needed national cultural center in the capital city. Today, the JFK Center for the Performing Arts is one of the leading cultural institutions in the country. The center is unique in its dual role as memorial to a much-loved president and as an active cultural center, and is as such "a living memorial." There are as many visitors to the Center for the Performing Arts each year as to the Capitol or the Air and Space Museum.

Edward Durrel Stone, *Architect,* was one of the leaders of modern architecture.

The site along the banks of the Potomac River is outside the organized grid of L'Enfant's planned city and unfortunately encircled by highways and other large, unrelated buildings. The low, rectangular Center is surrounded on all sides by a metal colonnade and is clad in white Carrara marble (a gift from Italy). The massing of the building and the materials used clearly echo the *Neoclassical* Lincoln Memorial visible down the river. Spanning the entire length of the river facade, the Grand Foyer (630 feet long x 40 feet wide x 60 feet high) is arguably the largest room in the world. Floor-to-ceiling mirrors (a gift from Belgium) face the floor-to-ceiling glass overlooking the terrace. The eighteen Orrefors crystal chandeliers were a gift form Sweden. In the center of the foyer is a seven-foot-high bronze bust of John F. Kennedy by **Robert Berks,** *Sculptor.*

The Hall of Nations displays flags from foreign countries and the Hall of States displays flags of the 50 states. These long, narrow spaces separate the three principle theaters housed in the center.

"And so, my fellow Americans,
  ask not what your country can do for you;
  ask what you can do for your country."

JOHN FITZGERALD KENNEDY
1961

*"Man has always gone where he has been able to go.
It is that simple. He will continue pushing back his frontier,
no matter how far it may carry him from his homeland."*

MICHAEL COLLINS,
The National Air and Space Museum's first director and astronaut, 1969

NATIONAL AIR AND SPACE MUSEUM
Milestones of Flight
SIXTH STREET AND INDEPENDENCE AVENUE, N.W.

The National Air and Space Museum celebrates the development and exploration of aircraft, rockets, and spacecraft. The museum first opened in July, 1976 for the country's bicentennial celebration. Today the Air and Space Museum is a division of the Smithsonian Institution and is the world's most popular museum, with ten million visitors annually.

The Chinese Imperial Commission donated a collection of kites after the Philadelphia Centennial Exposition of 1876, starting the Smithsonian Institution's aeronautical collection. The National Air Museum was established in 1946 and the museum's focus expanded in 1966 to include space exploration and development.

Gyo Obata, *Architect,* of Hellmuth, Obata and Kassabaum, completed the building within the four-year schedule and under budget.

The three-city-block-long building (685 feet x 225 feet) is constructed of seven boxlike bays; four solid bays, clad in pink Tennessee marble, alternating with three glass bays. The glass bays flood with daylight to give the feeling of being outdoors. Steel framing and tubular trusses support the hanging airplanes as though in flight. The marble used in the solid bays is the same as that used in the National Gallery of Art directly on axis across the Mall.

The museum's collection of air and space artifacts is the most comprehensive in the country and includes many originals. Displays include the Wright Brothers' *Flyer,* which made the first successful human flight ever in 1903, and the *Apollo 11* command module, *Columbia,* part of the first moon landing. The museum has 23 galleries, a library, and an IMAX theater with a five-story screen showing films about flight. The museum's Albert Einstein planetarium has the most technically advanced equipment in the world, a Zeiss VI, donated by Germany. The three main exhibit halls are designated Milestones of Flight, Air Transportation, and Space Hall. Two massive murals, *Earthflight Environment* by Eric Sloan and *The Space Mural—A cosmic View* by Robert McCall grace the building's interior.

National Gallery of Art
East Building
Fourth Street and Constitution Avenue, N.W.

Andrew Mellon had the foresight in 1940 to reserve the site next to the National Gallery of Art (West Building) for future expansion. In only 30 years, the Gallery's art collection outgrew the West Building and through the generosity of Andrew Mellon's children, the East Building was built and opened in 1978. This powerful museum anchors the northwest corner of the Mall and is Washington's first modern building.

I.M. Pei & Partners, *Architects,* used the difficult trapezoidal site as the inspiration for the two interlocking triangles that create the building's distinctive and dynamic form. Despite the sculptured dynamics of the East Building, it harmonizes with the West Building with its similar clean, bold surfaces and pink Tennessee marble. The marble for each building was quarried from the same location and employs the same two-foot-by-five-foot module. The southwest corner of the building comes to a 19 degree blade-edge point; from the right vantage, the point gives the illusion of being paper-thin.

Entering from the plaza at Fourth Street, the visitor passes through a low, condensed space before entering the multi-story, sun-filled atrium. This grand public space is a series of interlocking triangles intersected by balconies and bridges from which the galleries are accessed. The museum showcases temporary exhibits, and new walls are constructed in the galleries for practically every new show.

Much of the art was commissioned specifically for the museum, including Henry Moore's sculpture at the entry, Joan Miró's tapestry, and Alexander Calder's 28-foot-high mobile in the atrium. The museum's collection includes great 20th-century masters such as Kandinsky, Matisse, Brancusi, Picasso, O'Keefe, Moore, Miró, Rothko, and Gorky. All the art in the collection, as well as the $95 million for construction, was privately donated.

The larger of the two main triangles houses the atrium, public exhibition galleries, and auditorium. The administration offices and the Center for Advanced Study in the Visual Arts are located in the smaller triangle. The glass trapezoidal shapes in the plaza are skylights over the concourse connecting the East and West Building.

*"...a palatial statement of the creative accommodation
of contemporary art and architecture...the finest
that informed connoisseurship and discriminating
wealth can buy."*

Ada Louise Huxtable,
New York Times, 1978

"The abstraction of the design permits each viewer to interpret
the war's meaning in a deeply personal way, in essence making it not
a single memorial, but a unique one for all who experience it."

Jury Comment, American Institute of Architects,
1984

VIETNAM VETERAN'S MEMORIAL

A Symbol of Healing

CONSTITUTIONAL GARDENS, N.W.

The Memorial was dedicated Veteran's Day, 1982, after a 48 hour vigil at the Washington Cathedral where all the names on the Memorial were read aloud. Congress authorized the two-acre site, located on the west corner of Constitution Gardens, for the Memorial and the funds were privately raised mainly through the efforts of Vietnam veteran **Jan Scruggs**.

Maya Ying Lin, *Architect,* was a 21-year-old architectural student at Yale University when she won the competition. The jury of eight architects and landscape architects unanimously picked her design out of over 1,400 entries, the largest number of submissions for such a competition.

The black granite Memorial is set into the earth and is inscribed with the names of the 58,183 soldiers missing or killed in the war. Its two 200-foot-long walls form a striking "V" whose ends align with the Lincoln Memorial to the southwest and the Washington monument to the southeast. Next to each name is a cross (signifying missing) or a diamond (confirmed dead). The highly polished granite reflects the faces of those who visit the Memorial. Many visitors make rubbings of the names or leave mementos such as purple hearts, drawings, letters, and photographs. The mementos are collected, logged, and preserved by the National Park Service. Over 10,000 people visit the Memorial each day.

Although Lin's submission met all the required criteria—to be "reflective and contemplative in character" and to avoid being political—the Memorial's design caused much controversy. This was not unexpected, however, since the Vietnam War was the most controversial war in American history. The Memorial departs radically from the traditional war memorial: it is not towering, white, and glorifying, but rather understated, below grade, and thought provoking. The abstract simplicity is powerful and moving.

To help appease the criticism, a realistic bronze statuary group of three soldiers by **Frederick Hart,** *Sculptor,* was installed in 1984. Located 100 yards from the black granite wall, the soldiers appear to gaze out onto the wall from a grove of trees.

BIBLIOGRAPHY

A FEW OF THE PRIMARY SOURCES USED FOR RESEARCHING
THE ARCHITECTURE AND HISTORY OF WASHINGTON, DC:

Washington Architecture, 1791–1861
Daniel D. Reiff

Washington Itself
E. J. Applewhite

The Architecture of the United States
G. E. Kidder Smith

Washington, DC
Michelin Travel Publications

*Walking Tours of Old Washington
and Alexandria*
Paul Hogarth

Downtown Urban Renewal Area Landmarks
National Capitol Planning Commission

*Washington, D.C.
A Guide to the Nation's Capitol*
Randall Bond Truett, editor

Washington, Then and Now
Charles Suddarth Kelly

The District of Columbia
TimeLife Books

Washington, D.C. Museums
Betty Ross

This edition published by DOVETAIL BOOKS.

1993 DOVETAIL BOOKS

ISBN 0-9636673-1-9

Printed and bound in Singapore

9 8 7 6 5 4 3 2 1

TOWN
New hampshire
Connecticut
Avenue
Rhode
Vermont
Mafsa
York
Pennsylva
Virginia
President's House
New
POTOMAC
WITHIN THE
the